The Language of Love

Collection

Dr. Yvonne Henderson

The Language of Love Collection
copyright © 2022 by Dr. Yvonne Henderson

All rights reserved. No part of this publication may be reproduced, distributed, or transmitted in any form or by any means, including photocopying, recording, or other electronic or mechanical methods, without the prior written permission of the publisher, except in the case of brief quotations embodied in critical reviews and certain other noncommercial uses permitted by copyright laws.

Unless otherwise indicated, scripture references are from the King James Bible Version.

Transitions Publishing
Missouri City, TX 77489

Preface

In October of 2021 I was confirmed a prophet and appointed as the Lead Pastor of The Love Church Houston that would be launched February 26, 2022. After my appointment I was given the task of teaching a Bible Study as were the other three Love Churches (Denver, Lima and New York). We were asked to teach on love seeing our founding scripture is:

John3:16 – For God so loved the world, that He gave His only begotten Son, that whosoever believeth on Him should not parish, but have ever lasting life.

Wanting to do something more extensive I asked God for direction, and He led me to what you are about to read. I found more than one type of love. There are eight; Agape, Eros, Philia, Mania, Pragma, Ludus, Storge and Philantia. In this eight-book series I will describe each type of love and reveal the scriptures that go with them. These books may be read in any order, and I pray as you read you begin to better understand the language of love.

Introduction

The study of love – I found in my studies that the Ancient Greeks have anywhere between four to eight different words for love (depending on the source).

Each one carries its own characteristics, which sets them apart from one another, so not to be confused as to what type of love you are exemplifying.

Table of Contents

Agape - Unconditional love, divine, selfless

Philia - Brotherly love

Bonus Chapter

Storge - Affection

Eros - Sexual, erotic love

Bonus Chapter

Ludus - Flirtations, Playful, Casual love

Pragma - Committed, Long-standing love

Bonus Chapter

Philautia – Self-love

Mania – Obsessive, Possessive Addictive, Dependent

Bonus Chapter

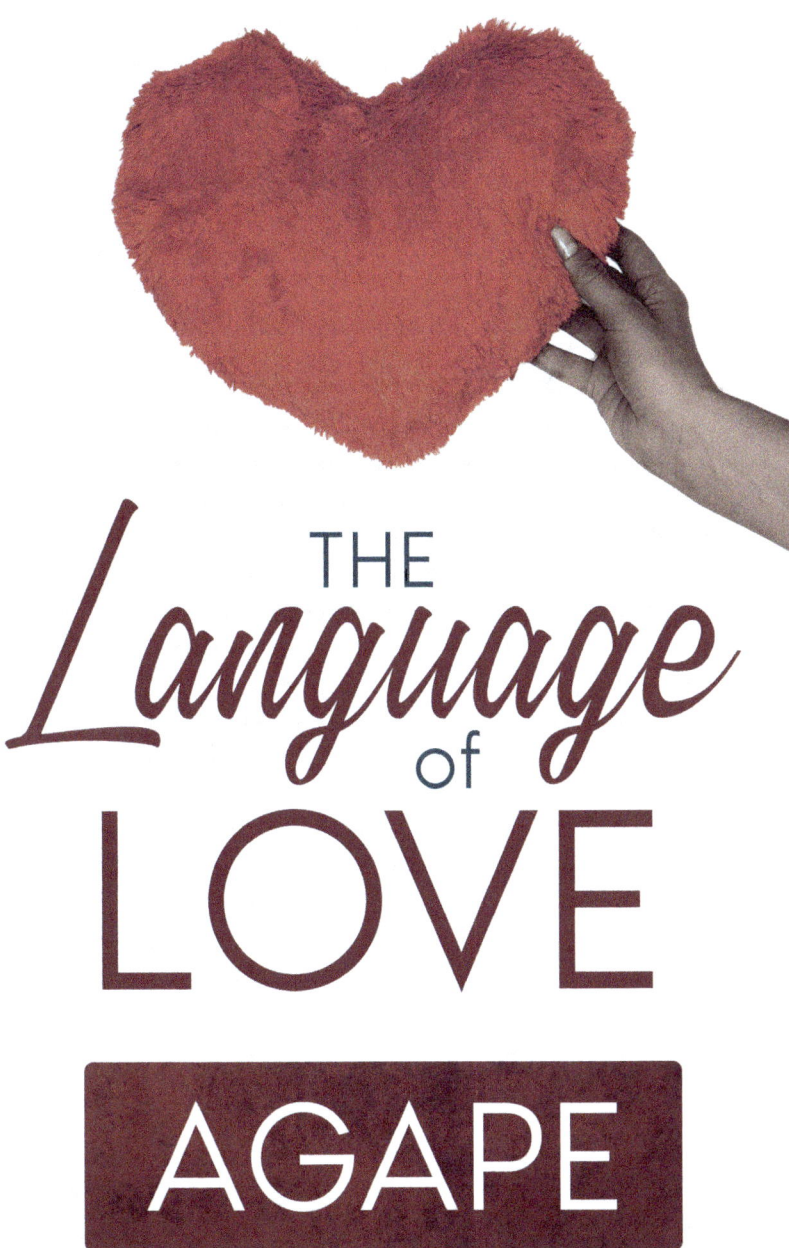

— AGAPE —

SELFLESS LOVE
An empathetic attitude of love for everyone and anyone.

LOVE CATALYST Spirit

WAYS TO SHOW THIS LOVE
Express unconditional love in any situation.

Agape Love

Love is and always has been a complex concept. It is an emotion, a state of being, a choice, an ability, a gift, a force, or all the above.

In English the word love has been used in reference to a "strong affection for another" since before the 12th Century according to Webster. It has been said it only has one word for love, but they have words that imply love, like affection, friendship, attraction, etc. The word love is constantly evolving with ever-broadening definitions. Human love therefore cannot be simply defined as it is being redefined all the time.

Which is why I want to talk about Agape love. Unconditional love, God's love is never changing. If God's love is never changing, it's the same today as it was yesterday, and it will be the same tomorrow. God's love is constant, it will do just what He said it will do. Let's look at *John 3:16* – For God so loved the world that He gave His only begotten Son that whosoever believeth in Him should not parish but have everlasting life.

What is agape love? It is something we do not deserve. I feel we may need out of state accomplishments beautifully described in I Corinthians 13, which is referred to as the love chapter of the Bible.

It tells us how to love one another as God did.

The word Agape outside of the New Testament has a variety of meanings, but when you see it used in the New Testament it is referring to how God loves. His very nature is to love, God is love *1 John 4:8* tells us that he who does not love does not know God, for God is love. Everything God does flows from His love. We are also to love God with the same type of love. In *Luke 10:27* – He answered, "Love the Lord your God with all your heart and with all your soul and with all your strength and with all your mind" and "Love your neighbor as yourself." Stop kicking people out and turning people away because they did not do what you asked, or they did not do it the

way you thought it should be done. Stop putting your expectations on someone else.
Agape Love

    Let's dissect this scripture, shall we. God told us to love Him the way He loves us, unconditional and on purpose. When He said love Him with your whole heart, that meant that you cannot have any other god before Him. He is a jealous God and does not and will not share you with anyone else. That is good news because we all want to have that type of love, do we not? For someone to love you and only you. Well, where do you think we got it from? Exactly our Heavenly Father. He wants us to only focus on Him, especially if you are single. He goes on to say we must love Him with our who soul. I know you are thinking how can we do this? Our soul is our inner most being, the part that no one can reach, but God, Then He says to love Him with all our strength. Well, think about it. We have the strength to do whatever we want to, but sometimes we half serve God. So, to love God with all your strength that means you must put forth some effort into loving Him. When you love someone, you do it on purpose and you put forth an effort to show them you love them. Think about a past relationship or even a current relationship. You put forth effort to love that person. Especially, if it is a new love, oh we go all out to show that new person we love them. We text them in the morning, send them little special emails throughout the day, call just because you were thinking about them. Well, God wants us to do the same thing with Him. Talk to Him just because you were thinking about Him. Sing Him a new song. Start smiling just because you thought about something He did. Tell everybody about Him. Spread the good news about what He's done for you.

Then He says, with you whole mind. We should keep our thoughts stayed on Him. The scripture says whatsoever things are lovely, whatsoever things are pure, whatsoever things are of good repour, think on these things. These are the ways of God, so if we think like God, we will become more like Him.

*Agape Love is always shown by what it does. *

Agape Love is faithful Matthew 6:24

? What do you think love is?

_____
_____
_____
_____
_____
_____
_____
_____
_____
_____
_____
_____
_____

? Is love an:

Action   Feeling   or   Emotion

Circle and explain

_____

_____

_____

_____

_____

_____

_____

_____

_____

_____

_____

_____

? What is some evidence you must back it up?

_____
_____
_____
_____
_____
_____
_____
_____
_____
_____
_____
_____
_____

? What are some ways you can show God, you love Him?

_____

_____

_____

_____

_____

_____

_____

_____

_____

_____

_____

_____

_____

DR. YVONNE HENDERSON

THE Language of LOVE

PHILIA

PHILIA

AFFECTIONATE LOVE
A love that runs deep in true friendships.

LOVE CATALYST Mind

WAYS TO SHOW THIS LOVE
Exchange your beliefs and imperfections with close friends.

Philia Love

Philia conveys a strong feeling of attraction, with it is anonyms or opposite being Phobia. It is the most general form of love in the Bible, encompassing love far fellow humans, care, respect. and compassion for people in needed.

During my studies, I was looking up information on brotherly love and I thought, as I was told the story of the Good Samaritan was an example of brotherly love when in fact, I found it is an example of Agape love. In that book we see God's love is unconditional, no matter what you do, kind of love.

Philia is a brotherly love it is most used and exhibited in close friendships like a best friend forever (BFF). It is a generous and affectionate love for each other as they seek to make each other happy.

Some people may want to get all weirded out about this and think it is a same sex intimate and physical relationship, but that is not at all what this type of love is.

While it may be friends of the same sex it does not mean they are in a romantic relationship. This mindset in the world is what makes it so hard for people to be their true authentic selves and causes them to leave the church. I'm not going to run that rabbit right know, I will save that for another book.

This type of love is rare in the Bible, but the best example may be found in the relationship of Johnathon and David. Johnathon had won many battles, but this time a young servant boy by the name of David was sharing his victory and you would think Johnathon would be mad because he is the son of Saul, but the opposite happened, he was able to build a friendship with David. Johnathon gave him his fighting gear including his bow. Now, if you know anything about Johnathon you know he was a master archer and to give up his bow was serious.

Johnathon and David made a covenant, a solemn agreement that bound them together as friends who would support each other. I Samuel 18:1-5.

We claim to have Best Friends Forever (BFF's), but have you made a covenant with your BFF? Will you be there for your BFF when things go left? Some of us have a hard time being loyal to a friend, let alone going to bat for them when someone comes up against them. Especially, if it is a family member. How many of you would stand up against your own family for a friend? Blood is supposed to be thicker than water, right? So how do you stand for right when wrong is present?

Understand that this type of friend does not come along that often. As a matter of fact, you may only get one true BFF in your lifetime. Of course, you will have many friends that will come and go, you may even

have one or two that will stick around when the going gets tuff. But there is only one true ride or die, ace, confidant that you will truly have. The story of Johnathon and David exemplify that to a tee.
Johnathon first shows up in 1 Samuel 13 as a great warrior for his father King Saul.

   Do you have a friendship, or know of one like that? One where you are totally honest and open? One where you must be accountable to someone?
Now prior to Johnathon and David becoming friends Johnathon saw his father King Saul changing and not in a good way. Saul had been disobedient in what God told him to do with the Amalekites and because of his disobedience God rejected his Kingsley and rejected his rule over Israel,

which caused Johnathon to be concerned about the well-being of Israel. He saw something different in David, his faith, and his undaunted spirit to go up against Goliath. That was something they had in common, a strong faith in Jehovah, which was the basis for their friendship. Despite their age difference, they made a Pac and created an everlasting bond of friendship.

Their bond was David's protection because God had told him he would be the next king and by becoming friends with the king's son who did not have a problem with him becoming king but protected him from the king was just where God wanted him. God will allow you to be in close relationship with people in your adversaries' camp to be able to protect you from the inside. David had help in the inside that was working to see Jehovah's will be done. All friendships are not the same.

We must be open to who God sends us. Even though there was a great age difference between them their faith in Jehovah and their love for Him was greater. Then friendship withstood the test of time. Some may think Jonathan was disloyal to the king (Saul, his father), but he had a greater loyalty to God the Father and His agenda for the people of Israel. He never went against his father, but he spoke up on David's behalf on multiple occasions to try and change the king's mind. Will you go to bat for your BFF? Is your relationship rooted and grounded in the same faith? Answer the following questions to see if you are truly a BFF.

? Do you have a BFF? Who? What makes them a BFF?

_____

_____

_____

_____

_____

_____

_____

_____

_____

_____

_____

_____

? How did you become BFF's? Do they feel the same way about you?

_____
_____
_____
_____
_____
_____
_____
_____
_____
_____
_____
_____
_____

? What is some evidence you must back it up?

_____
_____
_____
_____
_____
_____
_____
_____
_____
_____
_____
_____

? What are some ways you show that makes you a real BFF?

_____

_____

_____

_____

_____

_____

_____

_____

_____

_____

_____

_____

love

BONUS CHAPTER

The Benefits of Love

The world says there are seven benefits of being in love:

Love may make you live longer, dependance for survival. John 3:16 – I need you, you need me, pray for one another. Fellowship with one another. Hebrews 10:25 – Feed one another, clothe one another, and provide for one another. John 21:15-20. You see even with what the world thinks about love, it is still covered in the scripture. God is in everything.

Love can help combat disease, your body is a temple 1 John 4:18, no fear, Isaiah 53:5.

Love boosts your immune system, Ephesians 4:32, forgive so you may be healed.

Love helps you look younger – I Corinthians 13:4-5.

Love can help you slim. Fasting and praying to take care of your temple.

    Love improves your mental wellbeing, I Corinthians 13:2

Loves improves self-confidence. Ephesians 4:2-3. A love tie – Ecclesiastes 4:12 – We must come together in love; most people use this scripture when it relates to a marriage bond and the love of a couple. But if I am not mistaken God said where two or three are gathered in My name, touching, and agreeing, I am in the midst of them. So, I do not have to be married to you in holy matrimony to have a love tie, but I just need a common strand to tie us together and God will do the rest. We need each other to survive.

DR. YVONNE HENDERSON

THE
Language
of
LOVE

STORGE

STORGE

FAMILIAR LOVE
Flows between parents and children or childhood friends.

LOVE CATALYST Memories

WAYS TO SHOW THIS LOVE
Show gratitude towards the people close to you.

Storge Love

Storge love, a love I had never heard of before now, but something we can all relate to, if you have a family.

In the Greek the word Storge refers to family love, it is a natural or instinctual affection, such as the love of a parent towards off springs and vice versa.

Storge itself is not mentioned in the Bible, but we see references of a family love in the Gospels. Matthew 7:11; Luke 11:13, speaks of an affectionate father who knows how to give good gifts to their children.

Luke 15:11-32 – The parable of the prodigal son. Some would say he didn't deserve anything else. He got what he wanted, and he doesn't deserve anymore. Well, if our Heavenly Father thought like that where would we be? So many times, we only come to God when we want something just like we do our family members.

This may not be you, but you know those who do. Those members who only call on you when they need or want something from you, then you don't hear from them again until they are in need again. Storge love helps you to put these things in perspective it is an affectionate love that you instinctively have for family, but this is family members who have a close relationship not those who are estranged from the family unit, or you do not know.

This type of love is for parent to off springs, that means your children, not all family members.

It is okay to tell someone no, especially if you do not know them, we must use discernment in our giving and helping. Example: When I first moved to Texas after having a family reunion and meet some new cousins, I got a phone call from someone I did not know. We were cousins, but I had just meet him. He proceeded to tell me how we were related and before I knew it, he was asking for money. I told him I did not have it to give and he became very persistent, me being who I am wanted to help, but Holy Spirit kicked in and said, "check it out first." So, I told him I would call him back after church. I checked around and found he does this with every new relative he meets. Of course, I called back and told him no. This type of situation is not dictated by Storge love because he was not an offspring of me. We do not have to and cannot help all family members.

In Genesis 10 Noah and his three sons had a relationship, especially Shem and Japheth because they honored their father when he was at his lowest and revealed himself, they respected him enough not to embarrass him. This is a prime example of Storge Love, for an offspring having affection for their parent by not wanting to cause him harm and treating them with respect. The instinct ability to protect their father from harm kicked in.

But then you have those who do not have that instinct, like Ham, he did not feel the same affection towards his father, because he looked upon him and laughed (Gen. 18:12.) There will be some intimate relatives that will not show Storge Love towards one another.

How many of your family members look at you and laugh when you are in a compromising position? Sarah laughed at God when He told Abraham they would have a child. Family may not always be in your corner, but we have affection for them. They may not always treat us right, but we have affection for them.

Look at the story of Joseph, his father loved all his sons, but there was a special affection for Joseph. Joseph being young did not know any better he had a dream he would rule over his elder brothers and decided to brag about it, and they tried to get rid of him. When they saw what it did to their father, they were sad. Showing that storge love for their father's feelings. They knew Joseph wasn't dead, they didn't kill him because they had some affection for him as well, after all, he was their brother.

Quick recap, they put him in a pit, he went to prison, then wound up in the palace and had to help them (his dream came true.) He could have been a whole lot of things, but he had compassion and affection for his (storge love) when they were in need.

The love you have for family, can be good or bad. It is mentioned twice in the Bible where the opposite happens.

2 Tim 3:3 - The disobedient generation living in the last days is marked as "heartless, unappeasable, slanderous

without self-control, brutal, not loving good." Again, heartless is translated astorgos, the lack of storge, the natural love among family members, is a sign of end times. When children turn on parents and vice versa, storge love is not present and this is dangerous.

Romans 1:31 – Without understanding, covenant breakers without neutral affection, implacable, merciful. To get a full understanding we need to read verses 29-32. This is where we are, the end tines. Their heartless people with no love for their natural family is why the world is in the state of chaos that we see.

The Bible tells us sons and daughters will rise ad turn against their parents. They will become haters of them, so this is or should not be a surprise to believers this is WOE!!!

We cannot be comfortable with the state of the world and the church. Stop to look around you, what can you do to make a difference.

The ultimate example is when God sent His son down to the earth for us. He died for us. Let this world know that His blood still works. We are still covered. He is still in the saving business and ready, willing, and able to love you.

? How many are in your family? Do you love them the same?

_____
_____
_____
_____
_____
_____
_____
_____
_____
_____
_____
_____
_____

? How do you feel about your family?

_____
_____
_____
_____
_____
_____
_____
_____
_____
_____
_____
_____
_____

? Can you develop a healthy relationship after reading this?

_____
_____
_____
_____
_____
_____
_____
_____
_____
_____
_____
_____
_____

? What are some ways you can show that you have this type of love?

_____
_____
_____
_____
_____
_____
_____
_____
_____
_____
_____
_____
_____

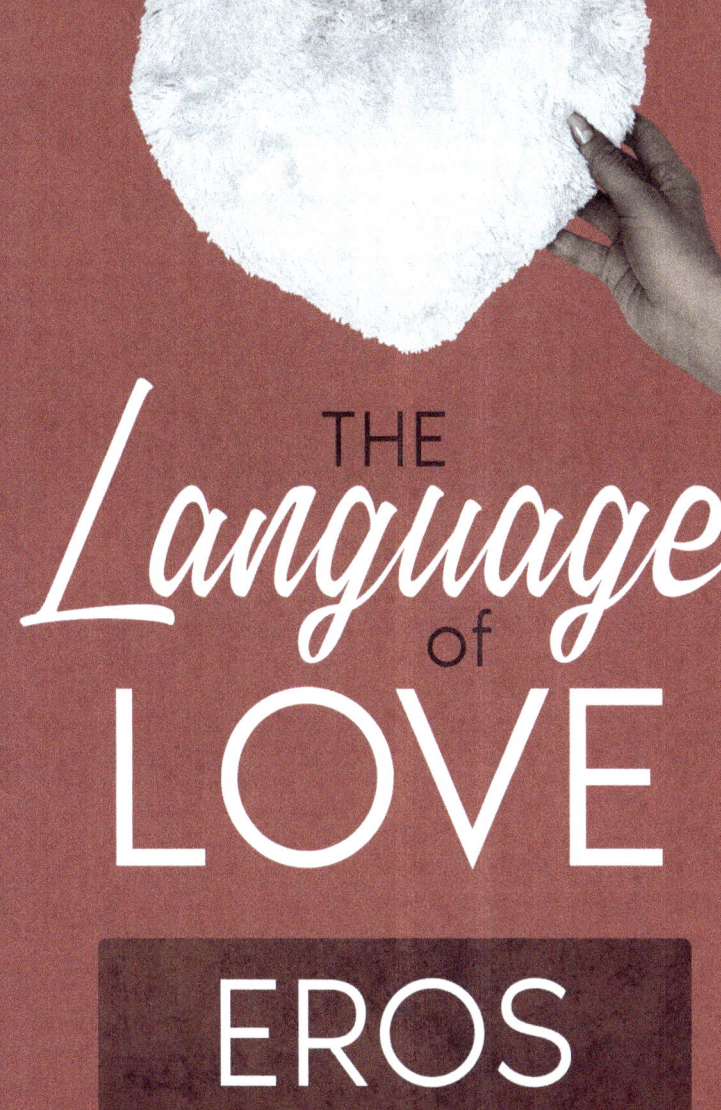

DR. YVONNE HENDERSON

THE Language of LOVE

EROS

EROS

ROMANTIC LOVE
Personal infatuation and physical pleasure.

LOVE CATALYST Body

WAYS TO SHOW THIS LOVE
Engage in physical touch such as hugging or kissing.

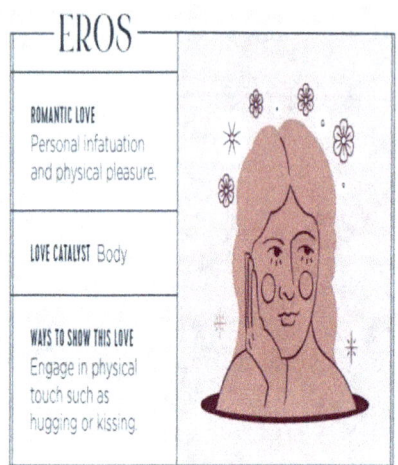

Eros Love

Eros Love is the physical sensual intimacy between a husband and wife. It expresses sexual, romantic attraction Eros is also the name of the mythological Greek God of love sexual desires, physical attraction and physical love.

Air ohs is a Greek term from which the English word erotic derives. The passionate, healthy, physical expression of arousal and sexual love between a husband and wife is the Biblical meaning of eros love.

The word is not used in the New Testament because it is Culturally degrading. However, it was not used in The Old Testament either because Eros is a Greek word and The Old Testament is written in Hebrew, but the concept is clearly addressed in the scriptures.

Within the boundaries of marriage Eros love is to be celebrated, and not used as a weapon. I Corinthians 7:3-5 breaks down exactly what that should look like.

> *"Let the husband render unto the wife due benevolence: and likewise, also the wife unto the husband. The wife hath not power of her own body, but the husband: and likewise, also the husband hath not power of his own body, but the wife. Defraud ye not one the other, except it be with consent for a time, that ye may give yourselves to fasting and praying; and come together again, that Satan tempt you not for your incontinency."*

Sometimes, men and women would withhold sex from their mates because they thought it was going to make him do what they want them to but, I am here to let you know that does not work. What that does is forces them or pushes them to function based on their humanness, to get that desire filled and that is one of the reasons that causes people to cheat. If you deprive an individual of something they are used to getting, no matter what it is they will find other means to get it. That is why the scripture said to come back together after a time so that Satan cannot tempt you. If we are totally honest with ourselves, some of us have very little control over our flesh when it comes to our sexual desires. We can withstand if there is no opposition, but how do you handle that same desire with opposition?

The scripture lets us know that once you get married your body is not your own, you are subject to your spouse and you need to discuss when you want to have a fast, so you can do it as a couple. Do not use that as an excuse not to have sex with your mate and ladies stop saying you are on your cycle every other week, you all need to communicate, so Satan cannot get into your marriage.

There are three things pointed out in this scripture you need to do within your marriage to ensure you have Eros covered according to 1 Corinthians 7:3-5 you need to

1. Submit – vs 3; Husbands give yourself to your spouse *{with*

good will and kindness} this is your marital duty.

2. Surrender – vs 4; Wives you do not have authority *{exclusive}* over your bodies, but the husband shares it with you, and same goes for the husband.

3. Sanctify – vs 5; Husbands and wives whenever you decide as a couple to set aside time for fasting, it must be mutual and not for a long period of time.

Eros love is not for singles, some seem to think that having a passionate love for a boyfriend or girlfriend is the same and it is not. You see the Bible refers to it as sexual immortality when you are not married, well what does that mean, I'm glad you asked. *Sexual immortality means the evil ascribed to sexual acts that violate social connections.*

In the New Testament sexual immortality is "porneia" also translated as Whoredoem, fornication and idolatry.
It means surrendering your sexual purity in premarital sexual relations. This word Porneia is Greek, and the English word Pornography derives from this concept of selling off. Sexual immortality is selling off your sexual purity.

For the single we must follow these same three aspects, but from a different perspective. I Corinthians 6:18-20

1. Surrender - vs 18; Singles, surrendering your total is hard, but you must surrender your mind, body, and soul to the Holy Spirit.

2. Submit - vs 19; Singles, once you accept Christ and invite Holy Spirit into your life, you are no longer your own. You are a temple for the Holy Spirit, and you must submit to Him daily.

3. Sanctify – vs 20; Being bought denotes that you are worth something and you were purchased with something

precious, *{the blood of Jesus}* So be holy as He was holy.

I know this is not an easy task, but it must be taught. As leaders we must make sure we are teaching the unadulterated Gospel, because we are held responsible for those who are lead astray weather, we did it intentionally or not. We must also be walking this way ourselves if we are not married. Yeah, I know I just stepped on a lot of toes including my own. Be blessed and seek to love the way Christ has commanded us to.

? Are you married or Single?
How is your love life?

_____

_____

_____

_____

_____

_____

_____

_____

_____

_____

_____

? How do you feel about your Eros Love?

? What may change in your relationship after reading this?

_____

_____

_____

_____

_____

_____

_____

_____

_____

_____

_____

_____

_____

? What do you need to do different to walk out your singleness?

_____

_____

_____

_____

_____

_____

_____

_____

_____

_____

_____

_____

love

BONUS CHAPTER

The Standard of Love
Luke 6:27-38

We all have standards that we live up to or at least try to. We have standards for how we run our homes. How we act and perform on our jobs, and how we conduct ourselves in the public eye. We find it necessary to act in a certain way, yet when it comes to following the standards of God, we seem to fall short. The world even has its standards for love; get yours before they get theirs, but Luke 6:31 says, we have gotten accustomed to living by that motto and think it is okay.

The world says be guarded, test the waters first, put in your pinky toe before diving in, so to speak, and make sure you always keep your heart guarded and protected just in case it does not work out. The world would have you walking in fear.

The world says, show them some of you, but not the true you. Talk, but do not give too much information because you might scare them off.

The world says have options, do not put all your eggs in one basket, keep something on the back burner for a rainy day.

The world says keep your distance, be ready to run at the first sight of trouble.

The world says care less, following the worlds standards for love will have you old and alone.

Luke with this letter to Theophilus which means "lover of god." It is said that it is a pseudo name for anyone who wants to hear, here in Luke Jesus is speaking to His disciples, but He makes it plain that the message is not just for the disciples, but for anyone who was a lover of God.

Jesus has laid out the standard of love we should have as lovers of God. If you say you love God, this is the standard by which one must abide.

Now the biggest problem is that not all will listen. Some will blatantly disobey the standard of love because they wan to. You have people in your houses, on jobs and in the world in general who will just not follow the rules no matter what you do or the consequences, they will have to face, they just will not comply.

Then you have those who will do everything in their power to follow the standard or rules set before them, even to the point of chastising themselves and punishing themselves for falling short.

Then you have those who want to follow the standards or rules but are always looking for an escape or loophole to keep from following it to the letter, they want to find short cuts.

I am her to let you know there are no loopholes in following God's standards or rules. His standards come with promises, so when you try to finagle your way around His way you miss out on the promise attached to the standard.

We have standards/rules for a reason; to keep man in line. The world has rules and standards, and we follow those for the most part, but are God's standards less than the worlds standards? I think not. For He says in

His word render unto Caesar that which is Caesars and unto God that which is Gods. We should not do anything that is contrary to the word of God. We cannot fall to the world systems and say I will lose my job if I do not do it. Who are you trusting man or God, if it is contrary to Gods word and you follow Gods standard, He is obligated to take care of you, just like He said He would, when He said I will supply all your needs through my riches in Christ Jesus.

The difference between the world and the Christian is that we cannot look at this scripture or rules to be obeyed, but a standard an attitude of the heart that expresses itself positively when others are negative. It is an inner disposition not a legal duty. The law had already been fulfilled when Christ came.

Vs. 29 – Know when to walk away and know when to fight. Pick your battles. This is not for the faint of heart. This is a way of life, not just a set of rules to follow. We do this daily. Christ said pick up your cross and follow me. We must dye to ourselves daily to accomplish the standard of love God has set before us. We cannot do this in our own might, but by the power of the Holy Spirit do we do these things.
Praise be to God for His word!

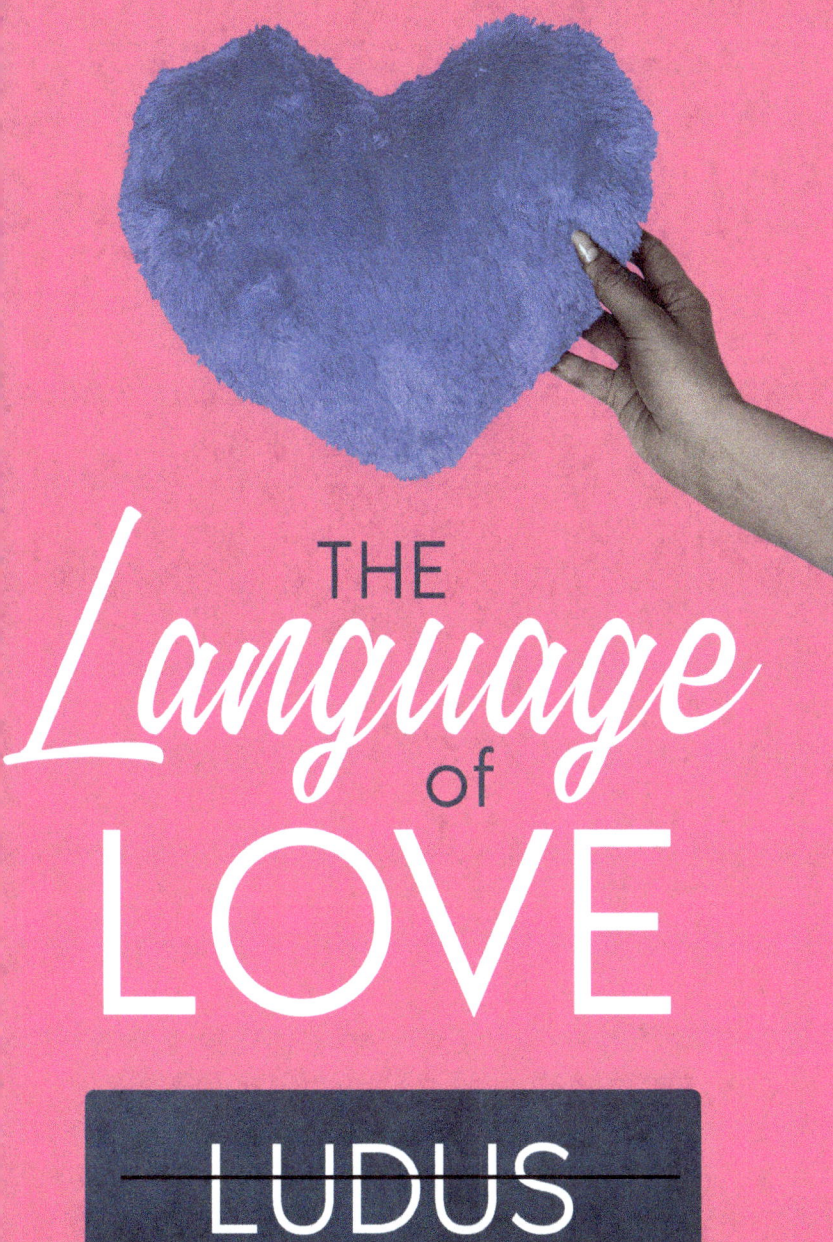

LUDUS

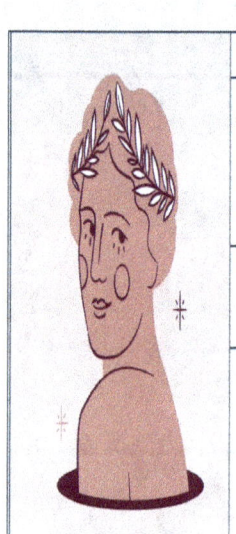

PLAYFUL LOVE
Flirting and beginning stages of intimate love.

LOVE CATALYST Emotion

WAYS TO SHOW THIS LOVE
Express a flirtatious interest in who you admire.

Ludus Love

    Have you ever looked at someone in a playful manner and may be made a comment to them and laughed about afterwards? Or maybe you were at a restaurant and was being playful with the waiter or waitress while they were taking you order? If you have ever done either one of these things you have shown someone Ludus Love.

    Ludus love is a playful or uncommitted love that involves activities such as teasing, dancing, or more overt flirting, seductive and conjugating moves. This love is not long lasting, it is for a specific time then it expires. When you flirt with someone it is just for a moment and it fades away.

Think about how many times you have gone out to eat and flirted with the waitress, waiter, server, manager, or cashier. What do you think it would look like if were to develop a relationship with them all? That would be absurd and unmeaningful.

Think about the way you moved on the dance floor when you went out; do not go too far back. Oh, do not act like you have not ever gotten close or maybe too close to a person on the dance floor, did some move or made some gestures that maybe were provocative to say the least and made you and the other person feel like there could possibly be more to it if you pursued it and it did not work, well that's because the feelings had expired shortly after they were expressed.

This is not the type of love you use to build a lasting relationship. Not to say it cannot work, but it would take more. One main problem to building a relationship on this is that it may be one sided.

The more flirtatious person, who probably does this everywhere they go with everyone they meet will not have that since of commitment that the other may be looking for resulting in a failed relationship. Some people are only attracted to this type of love which leads to one-night stands and friends with benefits.

You are so taken by the attention given you mistake it for an affectionate relationship. This may even create stalkers, which we will talk about in another book.

You may not think this is dealt with in the Word of God, but it is, The Bible covers everything. This type of love can be found in Song of Solomon, there are several accounts of Ludus love between King Solomon and his maiden.

In Chapters 2, 4, 7 and 8 are numerous accounts of the king speaking to his maiden and her responses to him. They are very flirtatious and erotic to say the least. Their flirting was on another level.

Example: Song of Solomon 4:3-5 **(King Solomon)**

"Thy lips are like a thread of scarlet, and thy speech is comely: thy temples are like a piece of a pomegranate within thy locks. Thy neck is like a tower of David builded for an armoury, whereon there hang a

thousand bucklers, all shields of mighty men.

Thy two breasts are like two young roes that are twins which feed among the lilies."

I am not making this up it is in the Bible. The words they used then were so elegant, it would put the wrap of those today to shame. King Solomon was a real one and I do not think anyone has created a better rap.

The Song of Solomon is poetry in motion, every word spoken is done so creatively and specific that it makes you quiver. Some of his spoken words are explicit, he gives a perfect example of how to flatter a woman and his maiden knows how to respond in kind.

Example: Song of Solomon 4:15-16 **(His maiden)**

"A fountain of gardens, a well of living waters, and streams from Lebanon. Awake, O north wind; and come, thou south; blow upon my garden, that the spices thereof may flow out. Let my beloved come into his garden and eat his pleasant fruits."

Ooooh weee! This right here would have anyone blushing, but just remember Ludus love is temporary, it only lasts for a moment then it expires. This is the kind of stuff that causes affairs, because you have someone telling you things you have never heard before and you are intrigued to the point of engagement, and it causes more harm than good. It is not healthy to engage in this for a long period of time because it will become misconstrued to one thinking it is real love.

Other forms of Ludus love could be used in love notes, romance novels, doing fun activities with your spouse, or just spontaneous. This is not the type of love you build a relationship on; however, you can use this to enhance one.

The sad part is that there are those who engage in this type of love and have never experienced anything else, hence why some have a problem with being in a committed relationship because they engage in a long-term relationship that were built on flirtatious behavior without substance.

? Are you married or Single?
- How is your love life?

_____
_____
_____
_____
_____
_____
_____
_____
_____
_____
_____
_____

? Reflect on a time you engaged in Ludus love.

_____

_____

_____

_____

_____

_____

_____

_____

_____

_____

_____

_____

_____

? What may change in your relationship after reading this?

_____
_____
_____
_____
_____
_____
_____
_____
_____
_____
_____
_____
_____

? What do you need to do not to fall victim to this type of love?

_____
_____
_____
_____
_____
_____
_____
_____
_____
_____
_____
_____
_____

THE Language of LOVE

DR. YVONNE HENDERSON

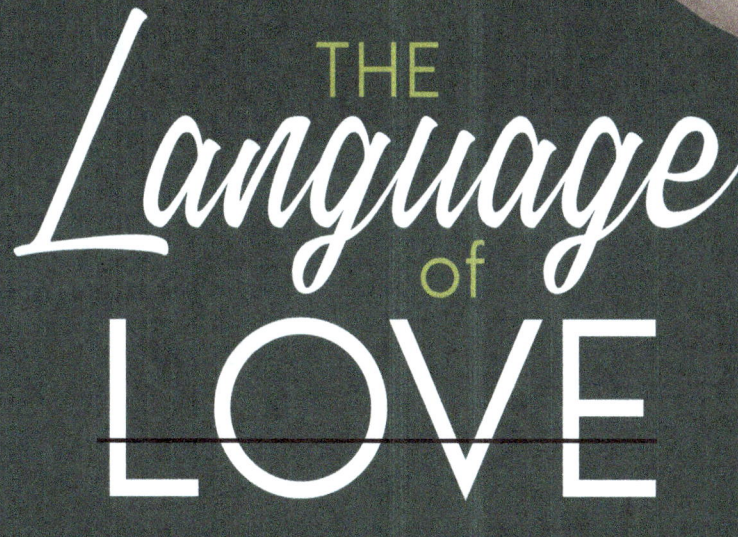

PRAGMA

PRAGMA

ENDURING LOVE
Mature love that develops over time.

LOVE CATALYST Subconscious

WAYS TO SHOW THIS LOVE
Put effort into long-term and reciprocative relationships.

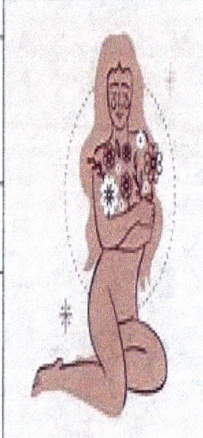

Pragma Love

 I hope you are enjoying this series, if you have read the others, if not you may want to get all eight.

 Pragma love is the kind of love founded on reason or duty and one's longer-term investment. Sexual attraction takes a back seat in favor of personal qualities and compatibilities, shared goals, and "making it work." In the days of arranged marriages, pragma love was more common than courting. Amongst royalty they did not have the opportunity to find and date people, they were betrothed to someone in a family with wealth or status to continue a lifestyle or a legacy. Feelings were not involved, they had to learn one another and grow to love one another, because love was not the main reason for the marriage.

In arranged marriages the groom had to present the family with goods to replace what was being taken from their home, to make sure they would be able to continue the lifestyle they were accustomed to when that person was in the home. The father giving the bride wanted to make sure that their daughter would in turn be able to continue in the lifestyle that they were accustomed to before leaving their fathers home. Not only continuing the lifestyle, but to better it where they would eventually have more than what they left with.

Some may think this is no longer the case, however, in other countries arranged marriages are still being done and they are expected to stay together. Only in the America's do we find this to be primitive, but when you look at the divorce rate, it is higher in the America's than it is in any other country.

During and after slavery there were a lot of arranged to ensure a continued population of our people. You had older men marrying much younger women, or should I say girls, because most of them were not of age, but it was agreed upon with the parent.

Even in the Bible we see the story of Racheal and Leah. The story of Moses and how his bride was chosen for him. It was said that the oldest daughter had to marry first. Another story we are also familiar with is the Color Purple with Celie and Nettie.

Though it may not have been based on anyone we know, it is a story we can relate to when it comes to arranged marriages.

It is said that pragma is the highest form of love; the true commitment that comes with understanding, compromise, and tolerance.
This is a love that is bound by two people. The scripture reference is Matthew 18:18-19 – Pragma is Greek for a thing done, a fact, a deed, a matter, accomplishing by regular practice. This is also known as enduring love.
This love values the practical aspects of a relationship as the most important driving force. A lasting bond, a commitment, a covenant.

The pragmatic lover looks at what values they want or find important in a partner.

Vs. 18 – Verily I say unto you whatsoever things ye bind together on earth ye shall bind together in heaven; and whatsoever things you loose on earth shall be loosed in heaven.

Maybe I'm the only one who did this, but I had a checklist of what type of man I wanted to marry, from the type of hair, eye color, height, skin color all the way down to the way he would walk and what he would sound like. The funny thing is I got just what I was looking for and it didn't last.

They say if you want to make God laugh, show Him your plan. See what we may want may not be what we need. I have gotten to the point where my prayer for a mate has changed to align with what God had for me and it may not look like what I envision, but I know He is not going to make a mistake. When I really look at it, it fits into the pragmatic love framework and definition, only difference is I have asked my Heavenly Father to arrange the marriage He has for me next time around. I am more focused on His agenda than I am my own selfish desires because He said if I delight myself in Him, He will give me the desires of my heart.

So many times, relationships start based on a physical attraction then a sexual attraction, what we would call the honeymoon stage, where everything is going well, then it settles down. You begin to learn those things you may or may not like about your partner. Some of these things would break up a relationship, but Pragma love seeks out a mate based on common goals, and capabilities for a stable sustainable relationship.

You may see some couples and wonder how did they get together? Or what in the world could they possibly have in common? These marriages are probably built on the pragma love concept or maybe it is true; that opposites do attract.

? What are you looking for in a mate?

_____
_____
_____
_____
_____
_____
_____
_____
_____
_____
_____
_____
_____

? Are there things you are willing to sacrifice for love?

_____
_____
_____
_____
_____
_____
_____
_____
_____
_____
_____
_____
_____

? What may change now after reading this?

_____
_____
_____
_____
_____
_____
_____
_____
_____
_____
_____
_____
_____

? Would you be open to try this type of love?

_____

_____

_____

_____

_____

_____

_____

_____

_____

_____

_____

_____

_____

_____

love

BONUS CHAPTER

Falling In and Out of Love

I thought of Alicia Keys when God gave me this title, but it is not just a secular thing Christians fall in and out of love too.

Revelations 2:1-7 – Jesus is speaking here, and He is speaking to the seven churches about what they need to do, so we too fall in and out of love.
He is bearing witness that they have labored and worked, they have dealt with the lies and backbiting of the people, and it has been hard, it has caused you to turn away, because you cannot handle it. You have tried Vs. 3 - people and found them to be liars not just any kind of people, but apostles, the real men of the cloth, but you keep on going because of Him, you preserved, you had patience. It is funny that

our Apostle (Cedric Wright II) had just mentioned this that we must be careful in these spiritual streets because people are willing to do or say anything to get close to you and draw you away from the truth.

How is it that this can happen – vs. 4 – you have left your first love, this is how the enemy attacks and infiltrates, he catches us when we are vulnerable, when we are hurting, when we have a disagreement with our leaders or family. The enemy begins to talk crazy to you, but I love Jesus because He did not stop there, He told us how to deal with it. He said, "remember" to remember denotes that you once knew what the right thing to do was. When you fall do not stay there and be used, remember from whence you came and get up.

See the enemy does not want us to get up, we must repent and do what we know to do. What brought you to Christ in the first place, His love, not man, remember that you do this for God not man, and there is a consequ3ence for not remembering. He will remove you. Now, I told you this is the season of Re- to do over or do again. You know what the first love was like.

To remember something, you must have first had it.

To remove something, it had to first be given.

To repent something had to have been done wrong.

Falling in and out of love is dangerous. Allowing people to pull you away from God is dangerous because you lose your benefits.

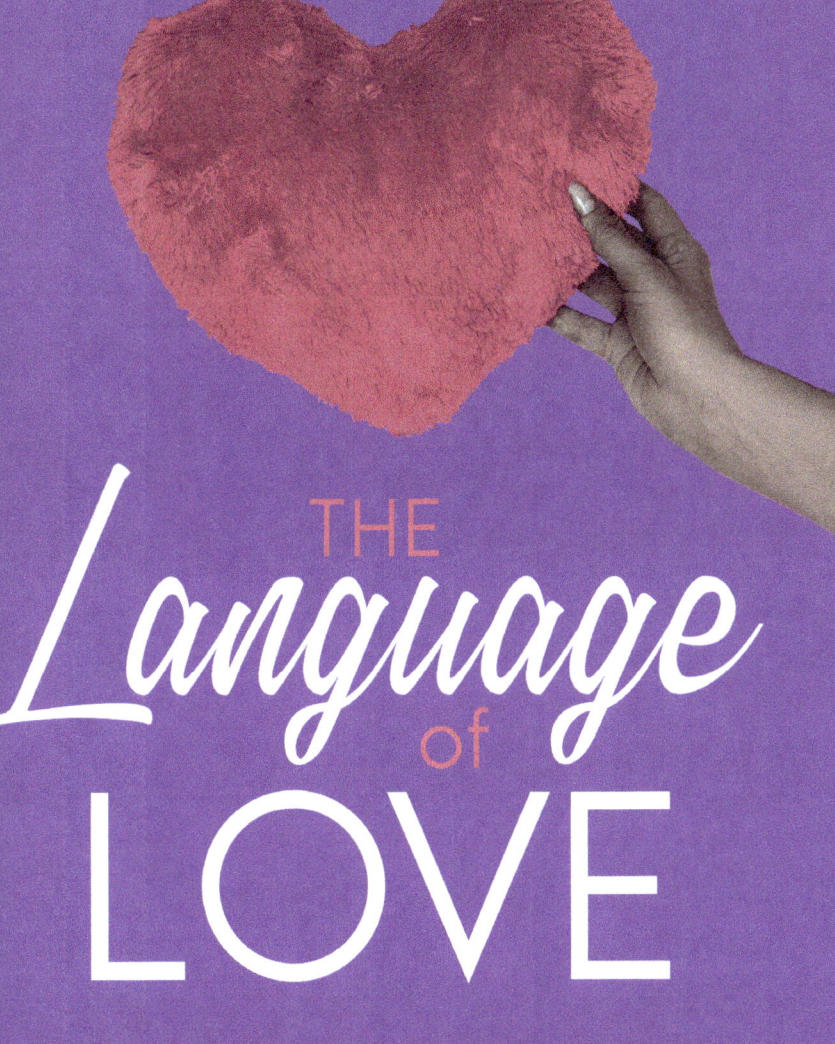

DR. YVONNE HENDERSON

THE
Language of
LOVE

PHILAUTIA

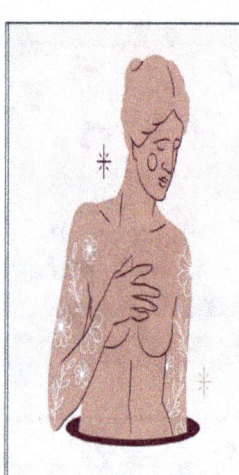

PHILAUTIA

SELF LOVE
Having a healthy "self-compassion" love towards one's self.

LOVE CATALYST Soul

WAYS TO SHOW THIS LOVE
Respect, accept and appreciate yourself.

Philautia Love

Philautia -*Fee loo thiea* love like Mania has two meanings. According to Ancient Greeks one form of Philautia was a pure selfish and sought after its own pleasures, fame, and wealth, which was very narcissistic.

On the other hand, you had a healthy kind of love for yourself, which is needed in any relationship because you cannot love someone else until you know how to love yourself. You cannot care for anyone properly until you know how to care for yourself.

So many times, relationships die because people do not know what they need, let alone want. People go into relationships with false precepts on what love is. If you have not read the other books you may want to. They deal with the other types of love that help you foster good love relationships.

According to the Bible we are to love ourselves, however, it must be balanced. You have some who love themselves so much that they will do whatever they have to, to be on top and stay on top.

You have people who will use you for their own personal gain regardless of how you may feel or how it will affect you. They just care about themselves and what they can get out of it. You may have a friend or two who only speak to you when it benefits them. Oh, but do not get it twisted you could probably think of some relatives who fit into that same category.

Sometimes you may see this type of love with children and parents. Children feel the parents are obligate to give them what they want whenever they want it. That is a selfish kind of love.
Then you have those who only come by or call you when they want something and get an attitude when you do not want to cater to them. I can speak on this because I have experienced it firsthand, and the relationships were one-sided.

We must learn how to have healthy relationships. What I have found is that when you allow people to walk all over you and just take from you, and you do absolutely nothing is because you do not understand what love is and how it looks in your life.

I am sure you have been in some relationships where there was a selfish type of love, that benefited only the other person and not both of you. I know I have had my share of those types of relationships. Until you know how to love yourself, you will continue to attract that type of love.

These types of people are called narcosis, this was depicted in the movie Squid Games, the person controlling the games was doing everything just to benefit himself and not the people playing the game. You can also see this in the Bible with King Saul was a narcosis. He was using David for his own personal gain until he felt like he did not have any more use for him. Then he wanted to kill him because the people were growing fonder of David than they were the king. People who are self-centered to this extreme are dangerous. Hence why Apostle Cedric has said many times, any ministry you become a part of that does not allow you to grow and move on is witchcraft or a booby trap. Do not allow yourself to become trapped.

Some people do not think you can do anything without them and if you stay under that type of teaching you will start to believe it for yourself, but God is not a man that He would lie, what did He tell you? How did He tell you to do it? He did not tell you to go into business with anyone, they just wanted what you have. Do what God told you and get from under their thumb so you can spread your wings and fly.

Why do we think we have to be in a relationship or partnership to do what we were called to do. That is a farce to keep you entangled in a relationship you do not need to be in, especially when it is one-sided. Release yourself, set yourself free and find real love.

James 3:16 says, "For where envy and strife is, there is confusion and every evil work."

When you connect with people or people connect with you that are envious, things will not go well. There will always be strife, you will always find yourself disagreeing with one another. We have talked about people only being attached to you because of your anointing, it is selfish.

In Proverbs 18:2 – Fools find no pleasure in understanding but delight in airing their own opinions. Selfish people are foolish, they do not listen or care to listen to anyone else. The delight in everything they say and believe they are always right.

The other half of Philautia (Fee-loo-theia) is self-love, positive self-love, where you take care of yourself by pampering yourself, take yourself out to lunch, to dinner, to a movie, go for ice-cream, or you may even take yourself shopping.

You do not have to wait for someone to spoil you, spoil yourself. I buy myself birthday presents; Mother's Day presents and most of all Christmas presents. Understand, that there is nothing wrong with you spoiling yourself.

Afterall, you show love the other person you love them right? You buy them birthday gifts, you celebrate them on Mother's or Father's Day, Valentine's Day, and Christmas. They have even come up withs significant other day and boyfriend and girlfriend day and grandparents' day. You treat them better than you treat yourself. So why can't you show you; you love yourself? Really, how are you going to treat someone else better than you treat yourself?

Proverbs 11:25 says, A generous person will prosper; whoever refreshes other will be refreshed, but the best scripture, that I love is the one that the Love Church is founded on John 3:16, this is the most selfless act of love ever performed. It funny or ironic that selfish love is depicted in James 3:16 and selfless love is depicted in John 3:16, and you think God doesn't have a sense of humor.

We must recognize and realize who we belong to Galatians 2:20 tells us we have been crucified with Christ and we no longer live, but Christ that lives in us. The life We now live is in the body, we live by faith in the Spirit of God, who loved us and gave Himself for us.

So, let's recap this: Christ died for you, so you could have a better life and you are living defeated because you are pouring love into everyone, but yourself.

The best way to show Him we love Him is to give up who we are, but we do, not want to give up who we are, because we think we are all that, when we are nothing without Him.

? What do you think about flirting? Should married people flirt?

_____
_____
_____
_____
_____
_____
_____
_____
_____
_____
_____

? How do you feel about your Philautia love?

_____

_____

_____

_____

_____

_____

_____

_____

_____

_____

_____

_____

? What might you change after reading this?

_____
_____
_____
_____
_____
_____
_____
_____
_____
_____
_____
_____

? Reflect on sometimes you engaged in this type of love?

_____

_____

_____

_____

_____

_____

_____

_____

_____

_____

_____

_____

_____

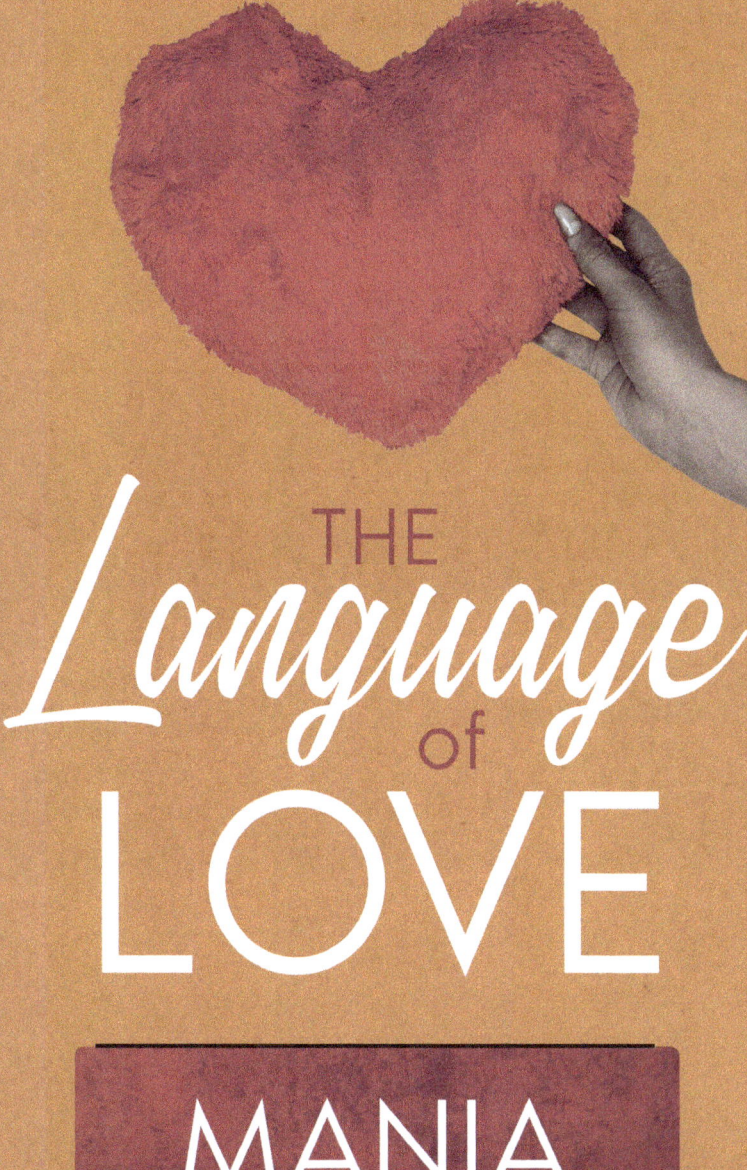

DR. YVONNE HENDERSON

THE
Language of
LOVE

MANIA

MANIA

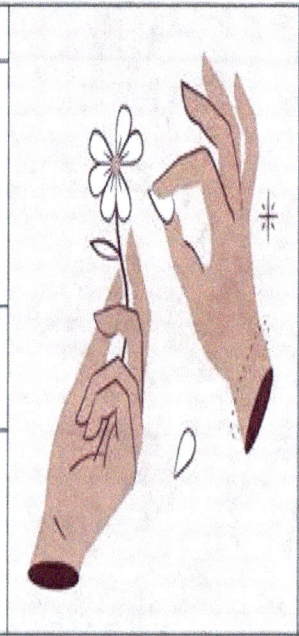

OBSESSIVE LOVE
Obsessiveness or madness over a love partner.

LOVE CATALYST Survival

HOW TO AVOID THIS LOVE
Focus on yourself more versus another person.

Mania Love

Mania love: sounds interesting right, well it is, it is so interesting there have been several movies about this type of love.

Mania is an obsessive or possessive love, jealous and extreme. A person with this type of love is unpredictable and liable to do something crazy or silly like stalking. Some movies you may think about are *Thin Line Between Love and Hate, or Fatal Attraction.*

When meeting a person, you must be sure that it is not just a physical attraction.

Mania love can get you caught up in relationships that are not healthy. Those who hook up and find that to be the only basis for their relationship will nine times out of ten it will end in a negative way.

Mania love causes one to have a false sense of security based most times on a one-sided love. Being the only one in love, in a relationship will cause one to become bitter and begin to do things that are out of the ordinary, like stalking someone to try and get their attention.

This will never be good because it causes people to be on guard and potentially call the police and file a restraining order to keep the person away from them. This will cause people to be on edge and always looking around to make sure they are safe. If they attempt to be in another relationship, they will have to protect their loved ones to make sure they are not in harms way. This is not a good way to live. These types of people will need some type of therapy.

Derived from the Greek Mania meaning mental disorder, from which the word manic is derived. Manic is associated with depression and other debilitating mind issues. According to Webster's Dictionary it is showing wild, apparently deranged, excitement and energy.
Manic love is a love flowing out of desire to hold one's partner in high esteem and wanting to love and be loved in this way seeing specialness is the attraction.

This love is found in couples who do not have the correct balance of Eros and Ludus love which causes Mania. With the correct balance of playful and romantic love obsessive love can be avoided.

Mania is a survival instinct. Let me give some ways to avoid Mania love:

1. Know and recognize the signs of possessive or obsessive behavior.
2. Do not act on them.
3. Focus on yourself instead of your partner.
4. Learn to trust.

Lamentations 3:22-23 – talks about God's love, but His love is healthy, Because He loves us so much. He is a jealous God, He has us consumed and in the passage consumed means covered, not burnt up. His compassions never fail, He showers us with it repeatedly. His mercies never fail, they are consistent 365 days, 52 weeks, 12 months, 7 days, 24 hours.

If we had to depend on another human to do this, we would think they were crazy, but from the passage wouldn't you say God is crazy. Everyone can not be crazy about you and keep it in perspectives, but God can.

We are consumed in His great love. His love is so strong and great!

? Have you ever experienced Mania Love? If so, what was it like?

_____
_____
_____
_____
_____
_____
_____
_____
_____
_____
_____

? Where you the one who loved or the one being loved?

? What may change now after reading this?

_____

_____

_____

_____

_____

_____

_____

_____

_____

_____

_____

_____

_____

? How would you handle a person with this type of love?

_____

_____

_____

_____

_____

_____

_____

_____

_____

_____

_____

_____

_____

love

BONUS CHAPTER

His Love Sustains Us an: Unsustainable Love

2 Corinthians 9:6-9 "Spare not" When I asked God what to talk about? He said my love being sustainable. I asked another question. God how does your love sustain us? He replied look at the notes in the notebook. How did He lead me? to 2 Corinthians 9:6-11, but I am only going to deal with verse 6-9, you will have to get the other books to get the rest.

This passage is very familiar to me, and it may also be for you. However, when looking at this scripture it was always associated with why we should give, but God showed me it is abut more than why we should give, but how He sustains us for our spiritual journey.

He made us a promise, give and it shall be given to you - Luke 6:38. The good measure He gives back to us is more than we could every ask, hop or think. Going is not something you just do, it is a lifestyle for Christians and if you have a problem giving, you have a God problem because by us giving His promise can be fulfilled if you do not give do not expect to get the benefits of the promise. Do not give based on the world's understanding because they do not understand the ways of God. Your acquaintances cannot expect to get the same benefits from your family as you do. They have not sowed into the family so how do you expect to reap benefits.

The first thing I see in vs 6 is your sustainability is conditionality. You may think well, "God's love alone is unconditional, but His sustaining love is conditional, vs. 6.

People in the world understand the law of reaping and sowing. Example – Farmers, investors and God gave the ultimate example of not giving sparingly, He gave His all for us, and we must follow this divine example.

Vs. 7 – Sowing has motives, what is your motive for sowing. The farmer doesn't worry about motive he can plant mad, happy, or sad and given that it is planted on good soil gets sunshine, and rain he will produce a harvest and make money.

Not so for the Christian – Our giving comes from the heart and how we feel about what we give and how we give must please God. We cannot be "sad givers" grudgingly or "mad gives" who give out of necessity, but "glad givers" who give because we have experienced His love and grace and can attest to His goodness. He who hath a bountiful eye shall be blessed. Proverbs 22:9.

The Greek gives us the word Hilarious for joyful. We must be joyful givers by asking God to work on our hearts when it comes to giving. He can still bless your gift if given out of a sense of duty, but He cannot bless it, if your heart is not right. Be a grace giver. Grace giver means that God blesses the giver as well as the gift, and that the giver is a blessing to others.

Your giving should never be about you, but how you can be a blessing to someone else. Ministry blesses other others that's why we give, not to pay the pastor a salary.

Vs. 8 – When you give with the right heart it activates God to start blessing you. Your blessings are immediate not prolonged. He is a right now God, He knows what you stand in need off when you give, but when you give with the right heart He immediately starts working on your situation.

The farmer must wait, but the believer who knows grace giving knows his benefits are not just long range, but there are some immediate blessings. That does not mean we will all be millionaires overnight, but He will supply all your needs.
The word suffering means adequate resources within. Philippians 4:11 says we have the adequacy needed to meet the demands of life through Christ Jesus. So why are so many believers running around

trying to find resources when they have already been promised to us?

Vs. 9 -

We not only have His grace, but His righteousness. We are righteous because our heart has no fear and it is sincere and obedient to the Lord according to Psalms 112:9 – Paul was not talking about us being righteous, but our giving because the only way to righteousness is by faith in Jesus Christ. God makes our character righteous through our giving.

Words from the author

I pray that something has been shared with you that will cause your heart to genuinely search for the true meaning of love. You may acquire a lot of things, but when you acquire love, you have acquired the greatest gift of them all. Faith, hope, and love, but the greatest of these is love.

I love you with the love of Christ.

Dr. Yvonne Henderson

Other Books and Journals follow me on Amazon

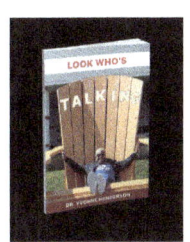

Transitionspublishing@gmail.com

www.ingramcontent.com/pod-product-compliance
Lightning Source LLC
Chambersburg PA
CBHW071244070526
44583CB00017B/2320